WHERE AM I?

This is a hot and steamy place.
It rains a lot.

WHERE AM I?

By Moira Butterfield
Illustrated by Julia Clay

Belitha Press

First published in the UK in 1998
by Belitha Press Limited, London House,
Great Eastern Wharf, Parkgate Road, London SW11 4NQ

ISBN 1 85561 786 2

British Library Cataloguing in Publication Data for this book
is available from the British Library.

Printed in Hong Kong / China

Editor: Honor Head
Designer: Helen James
Illustrator: Julia Clay
Map illustration: Robin Carter / Wildlife Art Agency
Consultant: Steve Pollock

Where am I in
the world?
Read this book
and see if you
can guess.

A blue butterfly
lives here. Can
you find it in
the pictures?

There are lots of leaves on the ground here.

The ground is a good place
for insects to find food.
Some of them eat leaves.
Some hunt each other.

The leaf insect and the
stick insect are hard to see.
One is green and looks like
a leaf and one is brown
and looks like a stick.
Can you find them?

It rains a lot in this place.

Lots of brightly coloured frogs live here. They love the rain. How many frogs can you count?

A spider has stretched its sticky web between the leaves. Can you see a rain frog sitting in a bubble?

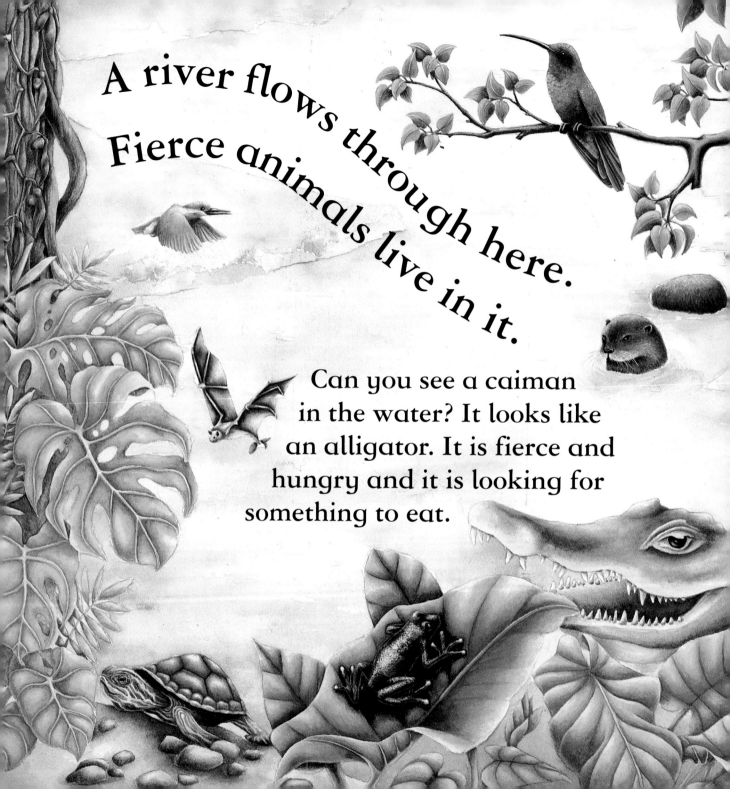

A river flows through here. Fierce animals live in it.

Can you see a caiman in the water? It looks like an alligator. It is fierce and hungry and it is looking for something to eat.

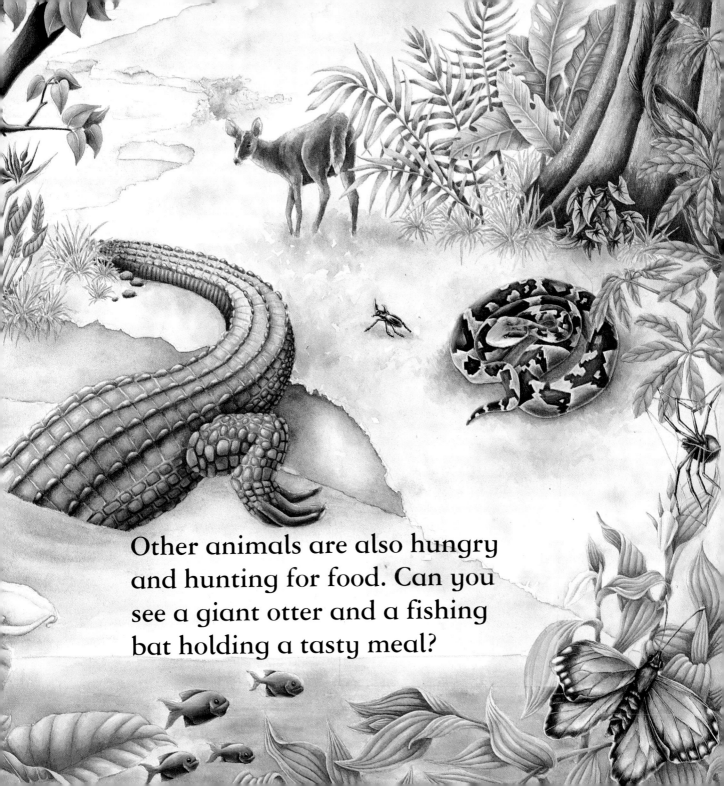

Other animals are also hungry
and hunting for food. Can you
see a giant otter and a fishing
bat holding a tasty meal?

It is very hot and steamy.

Lizards like it here because
it is warm. Can you see
the lizard sunbathing?
It is a green iguana.

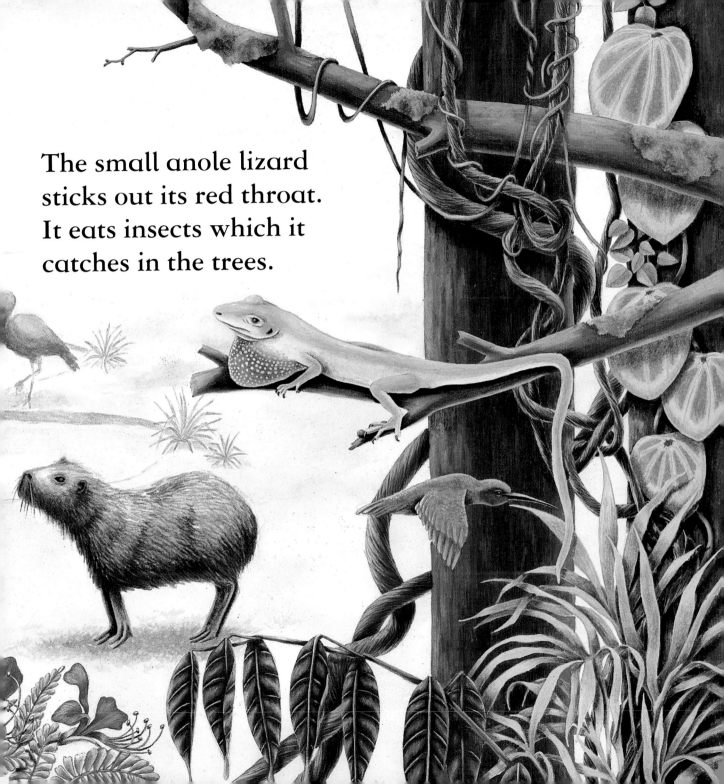

The small anole lizard
sticks out its red throat.
It eats insects which it
catches in the trees.

Lots of trees grow here.
Animals live in the trees.

The anaconda snake
grows as long as a bus.
It winds itself around
other animals and then
swallows them whole.

The spotted jaguar
sits on a branch.
It is ready to pounce
on anything that walks
underneath the tree.

Small animals climb through the trees.

The little green tree frog has big feet. It is good at climbing because its toes are sticky.

The furry kinkajou curls its tail around a branch to help it hold on tightly as it climbs.

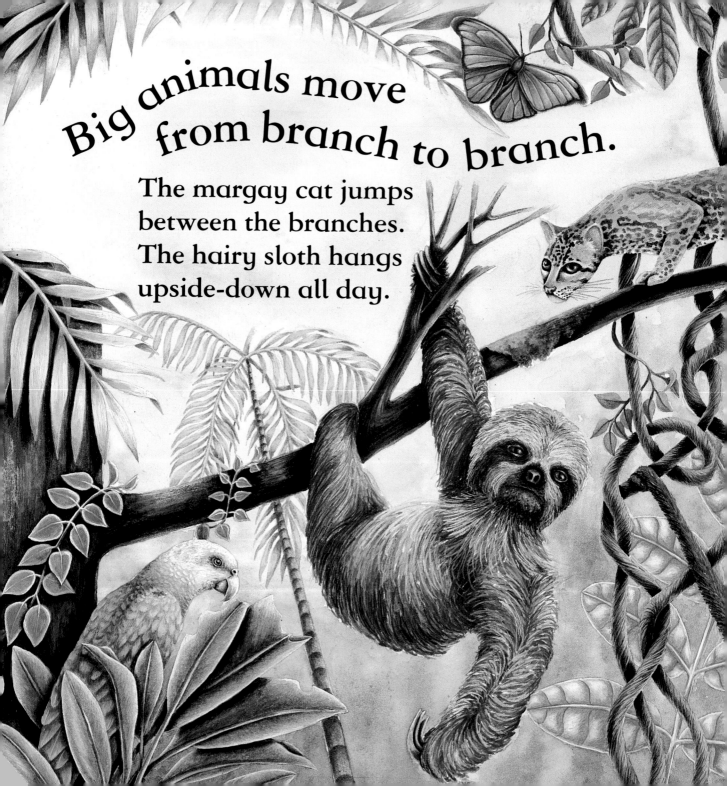

Big animals move from branch to branch.

The margay cat jumps
between the branches.
The hairy sloth hangs
upside-down all day.

Long plants that look like ropes hang down from the trees. Spider monkeys swing on them.

Different birds, big and small, live here.

Hummingbirds drink nectar from inside the flowers. It tastes sweet, like sugar.

How many birds can
you count in the trees?
Can you spot an animal
that has wings but is
not a bird?

Sometimes it is very noisy
up in the tree tops.

Macaws and parrots squawk
loudly as they fly around
looking for food.

Monkeys scream
and chatter to each
other as they travel
through the branches.

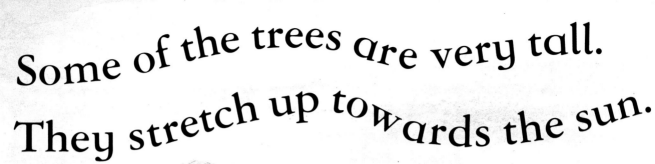

Some of the trees are very tall.
They stretch up towards the sun.

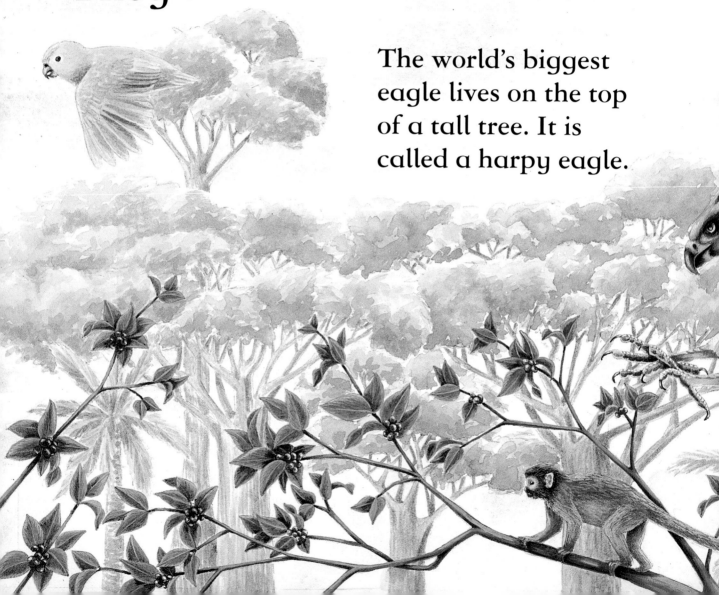

The world's biggest eagle lives on the top of a tall tree. It is called a harpy eagle.

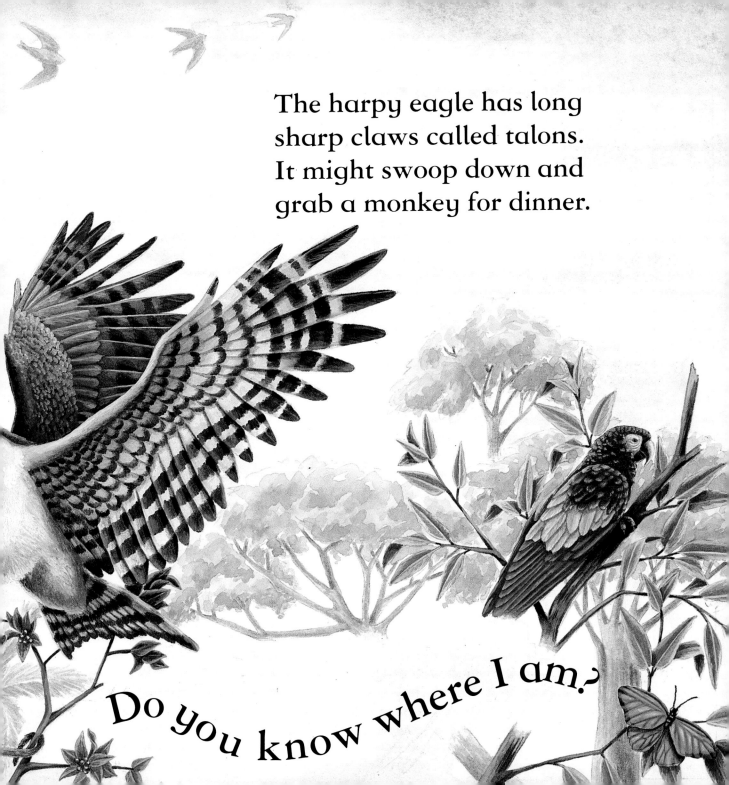

The harpy eagle has long sharp claws called talons. It might swoop down and grab a monkey for dinner.

Do you know where I am?

I am in the Amazon rainforest.

A rainforest is a giant jungle that stretches for many kilometres. Hundreds of birds and animals live in a rainforest. Lots of different trees and flowers grow there.

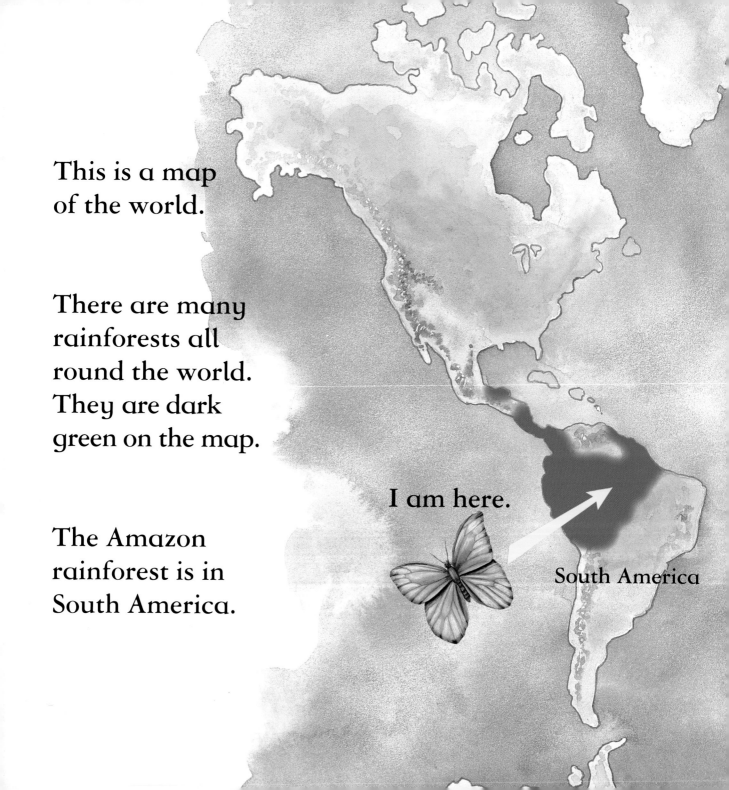

This is a map
of the world.

There are many
rainforests all
round the world.
They are dark
green on the map.

The Amazon
rainforest is in
South America.

I am here.

South America

Where are these animals?
Turn back the pages to find them.

Capybara

Turtle

Tamandua

Rhinoceros beetle

Toucan

Bushmaster
snake

Yellow-headed
parrot

Red brocket
deer

Red howler
monkey

Horned toad

Animal facts

The tapir eats grass, leaves and twigs. It pulls food into its mouth using its long nose.

The sloth eats and sleeps hanging upside-down. Moths, beetles and other insects live in its fur.

Pygmy marmosets are the size of an adult hand. They dash through the trees to avoid being eaten by birds.

The bat is a nocturnal animal. It sleeps during the day and hunts for food at night.

Armadillos have a hard body covering. They roll up into a tight ball when they are attacked.

Some poisonous frogs are brightly coloured. This warns other animals not to eat them.